PRESENTED TO

(*Keepsakes for the Heart* is an elegant gift collection that
includes a hardbound book with full-color artwork,
complementary bookmark, note cards,
and a charming box for keepsakes.)

Stories for a Dad's Heart

COMPILED *by* ALICE GRAY

Multnomah Publishers *Sisters, Oregon*

We have done our best to diligently seek reprint permission and provide accurate source attribution for all selections used in this book. However, if any attribution be found to be incorrect or lacking the proper permission license, the publisher welcomes notification and written documentation supporting corrections for subsequent printings. If you are, or know of, the proper copyright holder for any such story in this book, please contact us and we will properly credit and reimburse the contributor. We gratefully acknowledge the cooperation of other publishers and individuals for granting permission to use their material in this book. Please see the acknowledgments at the back of the book for complete attributions for this material.

STORIES FOR A DAD'S HEART
published by Multnomah Publishers, Inc.

© 2000 by Multnomah Publishers, Inc.
International Standard Book Number: 1–57673–695–4

Cover illustration by Steve Noble
Cover photograph by John P. Kelly/The Image Bank
Design by the Office of Bill Chiaravalle

Multnomah is a trademark of Multnomah Publishers, Inc.,
and is registered in the U.S. Patent and Trademark Office.
The colophon is a trademark of Multnomah Publishers, Inc.

Printed in the United States of America

For information:
MULTNOMAH PUBLISHERS, INC.
POST OFFICE BOX 1720
SISTERS, OREGON 97759

00 01 02 03 04 05 06 — 10 9 8 7 6 5 4 3 2 1 0

DADS

When God measures a man,
He puts the tape around the heart
instead of the head.

AUTHOR UNKNOWN

CONTENTS

CONTENTS

A TRIBUTE TO DADS

WHAT KIDS NEED
Marty Wilkins

oday's kids desperately need Dads who

...play catch, enjoy tea parties or wrestle because the heart of a child is there and they set out to capture it.

...laugh till their belly hurts and tears fall from their eyes while secretly creating deep friendships and memories that last a lifetime.

...make mistakes but consider them to be wonderful opportunities to learn.

...place an out of tune preschool concert or a ten-year-old's baseball game on life's agenda because they are of infinite worth to those playing.

...love at all times, because love is a gift freely given and not a reward for service well done.

...listen eye to eye and with both ears even if it means getting on one knee.

...admit when they are wrong and work to make things right.

...hear about those in need and say, "Let's do something to help right now!" and set off an uncontrollable wildfire of generosity and kindness.

...give the credit to others and empower those they touch to succeed in all that they do.

...model love as action, commitment, and truth even when it hurts because they believe God can work miracles in even the hardest heart.

...love the Lord with all their heart, soul, and mind and know that the rest is just details.

*The heart of every child beats
to the rhythm of a father's love.*
—*Steven R. Curley*

A Dad's Love

A GIFT FROM MY DAD

Steve Dwinnells

FROM *DECISION* MAGAZINE

I have a special box. It's a little, wooden box with two small, shiny handles and a tiny padlock. It's simple—no fancy engravings, no high-gloss finish, no felt-covered bottom. The edges don't fit together well, the hinges on the lid have begun to squeak.

But it's my box, and every now and again I take the small key and unlock the padlock. As I raise the lid, the box releases its special memories, and the memories take me back to another time and another place.

Inside the box are a few knickknacks and a letter. Not much value in the world's eyes, maybe, but a priceless treasure to me. This box was a gift from my dad.

One Christmas Dad made boxes for all three of us boys. He wasn't much of a carpenter. Some of the pieces aren't cut exactly right, and the joints don't fit together well.

But to me, a master carpenter couldn't have made anything better. The box's perfection isn't in its form, but in the motivation behind the making of it.

The box was made by big, callused hands that knew hard work;

by a mind that understood what responsibility means; by a warm heart that loved me. Inside this box is a handwritten letter addressed to me by my dad. The letter will never be published or nominated for a literary award. It is just a simple letter expressing a tenderness that Dad didn't know how to say very well verbally. It is a note telling me how proud he was of me and that he loved me. In the only way that he knew, he told me that he was glad I was his son.

Dad died a few days after Christmas that year. He didn't leave much money or a big home. But he did leave me that box. With a simple box and a simple message, he left me his love.

As the years have come and gone, the box has taken on even greater value to me as I have come to realize what it really symbolizes. It is a reminder that only the gifts of our hearts hold enduring value.

The smoothly sanded, varnished sides represent the hard work and the perseverance that I ought to strive for. The strength of the wood epitomizes the lasting strength that I need as I struggle through life's difficulties. The blemishes and the flaws reveal to me that perfection lies not in outward appearances. And like the letter inside, the box shows that warmth and love come from within, from the heart.

Like the box, I have nicks and rough edges, and my joints don't match up well. But just as a letter of fatherly love fills that box, I know that the perfect love of God fills me, making me a masterpiece.

I'M DADDY'S GIRL

Becky Freeman

FROM *MARRIAGE 911*

One evening not long ago, my husband stayed home with the children while I went to the grocery store. Shopping for a family of six when four of them are males takes a while, so it was late when I got home. When I walked back into the house, all was dark and unusually quiet. After setting down a bag of groceries, I tiptoed into the bedroom, lighted by the soft glow of the moon sifting through the window. Scott was lying there, his hands folded behind his head, staring at the ceiling. He seemed so pensive I immediately thought something was bothering him.

"Hey," I said softly and sat down on the bed beside him. "What's the matter?"

"Aw, I was just thinking about my daughter," he grinned sheepishly. "And how much I love her."

Evidently it had been a very good evening. "What happened with Rachel tonight?" I asked.

"Well," he sighed and searched for words to convey what he was feeling. "I had built a fire outside to burn some excess wood, and the telephone rang. It turned out to be a tough discussion with someone and I was upset. So I went outside to unwind by the fire, and, before long, our little girl came out of the house and snuggled by my side.

"'Dad,' she told me, 'you look like you could use a hug.'" He paused briefly and breathed a contented sigh.

"She's my little sweetheart, you know."

"I know," I smiled as I rubbed the back of my husband's neck. "And I hope she always will be."

The next evening Scott came home from work and found me asleep on the couch. He woke me by tickling my nose with a long-stemmed red rose. Before I could properly gush over it, Rachel strolled in from her room, beaming from ear to ear. Her strawberry-blonde curls boing-yoinging happily as she plopped down on the sofa beside me. In her small, slender hands she held a lavender basket of fresh daisies and pink carnations. Tucked into the arrangement was a card in Scott's handwriting.

"Thanks for the hug," it read.

Rachel's brown eyes twinkled, and she smiled triumphantly in my direction. "You just got one flower. Daddy gave me a whole basket!"

365 HOURS

The greatest gift I ever received was a gift I got one Christmas when my dad gave me a small box. Inside was a note saying, "Son, this next year I will give you 365 hours, an hour every day after dinner." My dad not only kept his promise, but every year he renewed it and it's the greatest gift I ever had in my life.

author unknown

DADDY HANDS
Susan Fahncke

I awoke in the night to find my husband, Marty, gently rocking our baby son, Noah. I stood for a moment in the doorway, watching this amazing man with whom I was so blessed to share my life, lovingly stroke Noah's fat pink cheeks in an effort to comfort him. I felt in my heart that something was seriously wrong with Noah. This was one of several nights Noah had been up, burning with a high fever.

Tears filled my eyes as I watched my beautiful husband move Noah's little cheek up against his own chest, so that Noah could feel the vibrations of his voice. Noah is deaf. Learning to comfort him has brought on a whole new way of thinking for us. We relied on our voices, a soothing lullaby, audio toys, and music to comfort our children. But with Noah, we need to use touch, his soft blankie, sight, the feel of our voices, and most importantly, the use of sign language to communicate emotions and a sense of comfort to him.

My husband made the sign for "I love you" with his hand, and I saw a tear roll down his cheek as he placed Noah's tiny, weak hand on top of his.

We had taken Noah to the doctor more times than I can

remember. It had been a week and a half and Noah's fever remained very high and very dangerous, despite everything the doctor or we had tried. I knew in my soul the way only a mother can know that Noah was in trouble.

I gently touched my husband's shoulder and we looked into each other's eyes with the same fear and knowledge that Noah wasn't getting any better. I offered to take over for him, but he shook his head, and once again, I was amazed at this wonderful man who is the father of my children. When many fathers would have gladly handed over the parenting duties for some much needed sleep, my husband stayed stubbornly and resolutely with our child.

When morning finally came, we called the doctor and were told to bring him in again. We already knew that he would probably put Noah in the hospital. So, we made arrangements for the other children, packed bags for all three of us, and tearfully drove to the doctor's office once again. Our hearts filled with dread, we waited in a small room, different from the usual examining room we had become used to. Our doctor finally came in, looked Noah over, and told us the news we expected. Noah had to be admitted to the hospital. Now.

The drive to the hospital in a neighboring town seemed surreal. I couldn't focus on anything, couldn't think, couldn't stop crying. My husband reassured me that he felt in his heart that Noah would be okay. We admitted Noah and were taken to his room right away. It was a torturous night, filled with horrible tests that made my son's tiny little voice echo through the halls as he screamed over and over.

I felt as if I were shattering from the inside out. My husband never wavered in his faith. He comforted me and Noah, and everyone who called to check on Noah. He was a rock.

When the first batch of tests were done, the nurse informed us that a spinal tap would be performed soon. Meningitis was suspected. Marti and I had prayer together with Noah. Our hands intertwined, we held our son and the love of my life lifted his voice to the Lord, telling him how grateful we were for this awesome little spirit with whom he had entrusted us. With tears streaming down his face, he humbly asked the Lord to heal our son. My heart filled with comfort and gratitude.

A short time later, the resident doctor came in. He told us that Noah's first results were back, and that he had influenza A. No spinal tap was needed! Noah would recover and soon be back to his zesty, tornado little self. And Noah was already standing up in the hospital crib, bouncing like he was on a trampoline. My husband's talk with the Lord was already being answered.

Marty and I grinned at each other through our tears, and

waited for Noah to be released from the hospital. Finally, in the middle of the night, our own doctor came in and told us that it was fine to take Noah home. We couldn't pack fast enough!

A few days later, I was cooking dinner. Noah was healing, slowly but surely. I felt at peace and knew my husband was the greatest father I could ever want for my children. I peeked around the corner into the living room and chuckled at the picture I saw. There was my husband, sitting in his "daddy chair," Noah in his lap. They were reading a book, and taking Noah's teeny hands to help him form the signs for the words in the book. They both looked up and caught me watching them, and my husband and I simultaneously signed "I love you" to each other, then to Noah. And then Noah put his little arms up, trying to shape his chubby hand in his own effort to sign "I love you" to his daddy. I watched with tears as my husband carefully helped him form his tiny fingers into the sign with his gentle hands. Daddy hands.

NOT ALL VALENTINES
COME IN ENVELOPES
Robin Jones Gunn

s a teenager, I worked as a waitress at a Coco's restaurant, in Southern California. Although California nights are supposed to be warm, on this particular February night the brisk wind shrieked through the front door. Around nine o'clock things slowed down and that's when I started feeling sorry for myself. You see, all my friends had gone to the movies, but I had to work until closing.

I didn't pay much attention to the man who entered the restaurant. A flurry of leaves followed him in. The sound of the wailing wind fell silent as the door shut itself. I busied myself making more coffee. Suddenly the hostess grabbed my arm. "This is really creepy," she whispered, "but there's a man with a white moustache over there who said he wouldn't eat here unless you were his waitress."

I swallowed hard. "Is he a weirdo?"

"See for yourself," she said.

We carefully peered through the decorative foliage at the mysterious man in the corner. Slowly he lowered his menu, revealing thick, white hair, silver-blue eyes, and a wide grin beneath his white moustache. He lifted his hand and waved.

"That's no weirdo!" I said. "That's my dad!"

"You mean he came to see you at work?" The hostess balked. "That's pretty strange, if you ask me."

I didn't think it was very strange. I thought it was kind of neat. But I didn't let Dad know that. Poor Dad! I acted so nonchalant, rattling off the soup of the day and scribbling down his order before anyone could see him squeeze my elbow and say, "Thanks, honey."

But I want you to know something—I never forgot that night. His being there said a thousand things to me. As he silently watched me clear tables and refill coffee cups, I could hear his unspoken words bouncing off the walls: "I'm here. I support you. I'm proud of you. You're doing a great job. Keep up the good work. You're my girl. I love you." It was the best valentine I received that year.

*H*e waked suddenly and completely. It was four o'clock, the hour at which his father had always called him to get up and help with the milking. Strange how the habits of his youth clung to him still! Fifty years ago, and his father had been dead for thirty years, and yet he waked at four o'clock in the morning. He had trained himself to turn over and go to sleep, but this morning, because it was Christmas, he did not try to sleep.

He slipped back in time, as he did so easily nowadays. He was fifteen years old and still on his father's farm. He loved his father. He had not known it until one day a few days before Christmas, when he overheard what his father was saying to his mother.

"Mary, I hate to call Rob in the mornings. He's growing so fast, and he needs his sleep. If you could see how he sleeps when I go in to wake him up! I wish I could manage alone."

"Well, you can't, Adam." His mother's voice was brisk. "Besides, he isn't a child anymore. It's time he took his turn."

"Yes," his father said slowly. "But I sure do hate to wake him."

When he heard those words, something in him woke: his father loved him! He had never thought of it before, taking for granted the tie of their blood. Neither his father nor his mother talked about loving their children—they had no time for such things. There was always so much to do on a farm.

Now that he knew his father loved him, there would be no more loitering in the mornings and having to be called again. He got up after that, stumbling with sleep, and pulled on his clothes, his eyes shut, but he got up.

And then on the night before Christmas, that year when he was fifteen, he lay for a few minutes thinking about the next day. They were poor, and most of the excitement was in the turkey they had raised themselves and in the mince pies his mother made. His sisters sewed presents and his mother and father always bought something he needed, not only a warm jacket, maybe, but something more, such as a book. And he saved and bought them each something, too.

He wished, that Christmas he was fifteen, he had a better present for his father. As usual, he had gone to the ten-cent store and bought a tie. It had seemed nice enough until he lay thinking the night before Christmas, and then he wished that he had heard his father and mother talking in time for him to save for something better.

He lay on his side, his head supported by his elbow, and looked out of his attic window. The stars were bright, much brighter than he ever remembered them being, and one was so bright he wondered if it were really the star of Bethlehem.

"Dad," he had once asked when he was a little boy, "what is a stable?"

"It's just a barn," his father had replied, "like ours."

Then Jesus had been born in a barn, and to a barn the shepherds and the Wise Men had come, bringing their Christmas gifts!

The thought struck him like a silver dagger. Why should he not give his father a special gift, too, out there in the barn? He could get up early, earlier than four o'clock, and he could creep into the barn and get all the milking done. He'd do it alone, milk and clean up, and then when his father went in to start the milking, he'd see it all done. And he would know who had done it.

At a quarter to three, he got up and put on his clothes. He crept downstairs, careful of the creaky boards, and let himself out. The big star hung lower over the barn roof, a reddish gold. The cows looked at him, sleepy and surprised.

"So, boss," he whispered. They accepted him placidly, and he fetched some hay for each cow and then got the milking pail and the big milk cans.

STORIES FOR A DAD'S HEART

He had never milked all alone before, but it seemed almost easy. He kept thinking about his father's surprise. His father would come in and call him, saying that he would get things started while Rob was getting dressed. He'd go to the barn, open the door, and then he'd go to get the two big empty milk cans. But they wouldn't be waiting or empty; they'd be standing in the milk house filled.

The task went more easily than he had ever known it to before. Milking for once was not a chore. It was something else, a gift to his father who loved him. He finished, the two milk cans were full, and he covered them and closed the milk house door carefully, making sure of the latch. He put the stool in its place by the door and hung up the clean milk pail. Then he went out of the barn and barred the door behind him.

Back in his room, he had only a minute to pull off his clothes in the darkness and jump into bed, for he heard his father up. He put the covers over his head to silence his quick breathing. The door opened.

"Rob!" his father called. "We have to get up, son, even if it is Christmas."

"Aw-right," he said sleepily.

"I'll go on out," his father said. "I'll get things started."

The door closed and he lay still, laughing to himself. In just a few minutes his father would know. His dancing heart was ready to jump from his body.

The minutes were endless—ten, fifteen, he did not know how many—and he heard his father's steps again. The door opened and he lay still.

"Rob!"

"Yes, Dad—"

His father was laughing, a queer sobbing sort of laugh. "Thought you'd fool me, did you?" His father was standing beside him, pulling away the cover.

"It's for Christmas, Dad!"

He found his father and clutched him in a great hug. He felt his father's arms go around him. It was dark, and they could not see each other's faces.

"Son, I thank you. Nobody ever did a nicer thing—"

"Oh, Dad, I want you to know—I do want to be good!" The words broke from him of their own will. He did not know what to say. His heart was bursting with love.

"Well, I reckon I can go back to bed and sleep," his father said after a moment. "No, hark—the little ones are waked up. Come to think of it, son, I've never seen you children when you first saw the Christmas tree. I was always in the barn. Come on!"

Rob got up and pulled on his clothes again, and they went down to the Christmas tree; and soon the sun was creeping up where the star had been. Oh, what a Christmas, and how his heart had nearly burst again with shyness and pride as his father told his mother and made the younger children listen about how he, Rob, had gotten up all by himself.

"The best Christmas gift I ever had and I'll remember it, son, every year on Christmas morning, so long as I live."

They both remembered it, and now that his father was dead he remembered it alone: that blessed Christmas dawn when, alone with the cows in the barn, he had made his first gift of true love.

People who really love each other are the happiest people in the world.
They love their children and they love their families.
They may have very little. . .but they are happy.
— *Mother Teresa*

QUIET EXPRESSION

He dreams, he plans,

He struggles that we might have the best.

His sacrifice is quiet, his life is love expressed.

Author unknown

THE GIFT
George Parler

It was our turn to open our presents this particular Christmas morning. The living room was already covered with torn wrapping paper from the onslaught of the children's eagerness to unveil the hidden treasures that had tormented them for nearly a month. Now we adults sat around the room with our presents at our feet, slowly removing the paper while at the same time holding back the child within ourselves and maintaining our dignity in front of each other.

My wife, Brenda, and her family have a tradition of getting each other gag gifts. This always makes me a bit uneasy at Christmas or my birthday, never knowing what form of embarrassment lies waiting for me under the thin confines of the wrapping paper.

One of my daughters, Christy, who at the time was six years old, was standing directly in front of me. The excitement of the moment just beamed across her face. It was everything she could do to keep herself from helping me rip the paper from each present. Finally, I came to the last gift. And with my natural Sherlock Holmes ability, I deduced that this had to be the gag gift. Because with them it was never a question of "if"; it was a question of when you came to it. So, with everyone looking on, I decided to go ahead and get it over with—just let them have their laugh—and I ripped off the paper. And there it was...a toy airplane about two inches long. Our holiday guests started giggling to themselves as I looked up to my wife with a smirk on my face and blurted out, "A toy airplane, give me a break!"

Brenda gave me the look—that look that always tells me I have just put my foot in my mouth and am in the process of thoroughly chewing it. I had failed to look at the name tag before I opened the present to see who it was from. As I picked up the paper from the floor and read the name tag, my heart sank. On the tag were scribbled block letters that read, "To Dad, Love Christy." I have never felt as low at any time in my life as I did at that moment. One of the most agonizing experiences of my life was having to look down into her little face to find the joy that had once been there replaced with a look of total embarrassment and humiliation. The fear in her eyes spoke her thoughts of hoping no one would find out that the gift her father found so repulsive had come from her.

This loving child had taken her spending money that she could have spent on herself, but she had chosen instead to buy her daddy a Christmas present. And it wasn't just any present. She knew from watching me play computer video flight-simulator games that I was fascinated with airplanes.

I quickly knelt down and grabbed her up in my arms and held her as tight as I possibly could, willing to give anything to be able to take back those words. I made a feeble attempt to explain that I thought it had come from Mom, but since I found out it came from her, that made it different. It was obvious that nothing I could say was going to change the hurt in her little heart. I had to find a way to prove I meant what I said.

And I did. I took that toy airplane in my hand and began making airplane noises. I taxied onto the runway, which was the counter, and throttled to full thrust and was soon airborne. My mission goal was to remove the hurt from my baby's face—that I had caused—and to continue until her smile returned. I played all day with that airplane. I put so much excitement into that airplane that the other children left their new Christmas toys and wanted a turn playing with my little two-inch airplane. And just like a little selfish kid I said, "No, this is mine!" It wasn't very long until Christy's face was beaming with a smile again. But I didn't stop there. That little plane became a treasure of great wealth to me, and still is, for I still have that little two-inch plane.

I keep that plane mainly because it came from my little girl's heart with love. But it's also a reminder to me of the power of words.

THE ONE THE FATHER LOVED MOST

Brennan Manning

FROM *LION AND LAMB*

A professor of mine once told me the following story: "I'm one of thirteen children. One day when I was playing in the street of our hometown, I got thirsty and came into the house for a glass of water. My father had just come home from work to have lunch. He was sitting at the kitchen table with a neighbor. A door separated the kitchen from the pantry and my father didn't know I was there. The neighbor said to my father, 'Joe, there's something I've wanted to ask you for a long time. You have thirteen children. Out of all of them is there one that is your favorite, one you love more than all the others?'

"I had my ear pressed against the door hoping against hope it would be me. 'That's easy,' my father said. 'That's Mary, the twelve-year-old. She just got braces on her teeth and feels so awkward and embarrassed that she won't go out of the house anymore. Oh, but you asked about my favorite. That's my twenty-three-year-old Peter. His fiancée just broke their engagement, and he is desolate. But the one I really love the most is little Michael. He's totally

39

uncoordinated and terrible in any sport he tries to play. But of course, the apple of my eye is Susan. Only twenty-four, living in her own apartment, and developing a drinking problem. I cry for Susan. But I guess of all the kids...' and my father went on, mentioning each of his thirteen children by name."

The professor ended his story saying: "What I learned was that the one my father loved most was the one who needed him most at that time. And that's the way the Father of Jesus is: he loves those most who need him most, who rely on him, depend upon him, and trust him in everything. Little he cares whether you've been as pure as St. John or as sinful as Mary Magdalene. All that matters is trust. It seems to me that learning how to trust God defines the meaning of Christian living. God doesn't wait until we have our moral life in order before he starts loving us."

No person was ever honored for what he received.
Honor has been the reward for what he gave.
—*Calvin Coolidge*

DAD COMING HOME
WAS THE REAL TREAT
Howard Mann

When I was a little boy I never left the house without kissing my parents good-bye. I liked kissing my mother because her cheek felt mushy and warm, and because she smelled of peppermints. I liked kissing my father because he felt rough and whiskery and smelled of cigars and witch hazel.

About the time I was ten years old, I came to the conclusion that I was now too beg to kiss my father. A mother, OK. But with a father, a big boy should shake hands—man to man, you see.

He didn't seem to notice the difference or to mind it. Anyway, he never said anything about it. But then he never said much about anything except his business.

In retrospect, I guess it was also my way of getting even with him. Up until then I had always felt I was something special to him. Every day, he would come home from that mysterious world of his with a wondrous treat, just for me. It might be a miniature baseball bat, engraved with Babe Ruth's signature. It might be a real honeycomb with wafflelike squares soaked in honey. Or it might be exotic rahat, the delectable, jellied Turkish candies, buried in powdered sugar and crowded into a little wooden crate.

How I looked forward to his coming home each night! The door flung open and there he stood. I would run to him, hug him while he lifted me high in his arms.

I reached my peak the day of my seventh birthday. I woke up before anyone else in the family and tiptoed into the dining room. There, on the heavy mahogany table, was a small, square wristwatch with a brown leather strap, stretched out full length in a black velvet box. Could it really be for me? I picked it up and held it to my ear. It ticked! Not a toy watch from the five-and-dime, but a real watch like grown-ups wore. I ran into his bedroom, woke up father and covered him with kisses. Could any boy possibly be as happy as me?

Later, it began to change. At first, I wasn't aware it was happening. I suppose I was too busy with school and play and having to make new friends all the time. (We moved every two years, always seeking a lower rent.)

The flow of treats dried up. No more bats or honeycombs. My father gradually disappeared from my life. He would come home with his hands empty. I missed him very much, but I was afraid to say anything. I hoped that he would come back to me as strangely as he had left. Anyhow, big boys weren't supposed to long for their fathers.

Years after he died, my mother talked about how the Depression had "taken the life out of him." It had crushed his dream of being a "big man." He no longer had money for treats. He no longer had time for me.

I am sorry now. I look at his picture and his crinkly hazel eyes and wish that he were here today. I would tell him what is happening with me now and talk about things that he might like to hear—politics, foreign events and how business is doing. And I would put my arms around his neck and say, "Pop, you don't have to bring me anything—just come home early."

And I would kiss him.

Love never asks how much must I do,
but how much can I do.
—*Frederick A. Agar*

43

GROWING UP

THE RED CHEVY

T. J.

FROM *SONS: A FATHER'S LOVE*

*M*y father loved cars. He tuned them up, rubbed them down, and knew every sound and smell and idiosyncrasy of every car he owned. He was also very picky about who drove his cars. So when I got my driver's license at sixteen, I was a little worried about the responsibility of leaving home in one of his beloved vehicles. He had a beautiful red Chevy pickup, a big white Suburban, and a Mustang convertible with a hot V-8 engine. Every one of them was in prime condition. He also had a short temper and very little patience with carelessness, especially if his kids happened to be the careless ones.

One afternoon he sent me to town in the Chevy truck with the assignment of bringing back a list of things he needed for some odd jobs around the house. It hadn't been long since I'd gotten my license, so it was still a novelty to be seen driving around, and Dad's red pickup was a good truck to be seen in. I carefully maneuvered my way toward downtown, watching carefully at each light, trying to drive as defensively as he'd always told me to do. The thought of a collision in one of Dad's cars was enough to make me the safest driver in town. I didn't even want to think about it.

I was heading through a green light and was in the middle of a main downtown intersection when an elderly man, who somehow hadn't seen the red light, plowed into the passenger side of the Chevy. I slammed on the brakes, hit a slick spot in the road, and spun into a curb; the pickup rolled over onto its side.

I was dazed at first, and my face was bleeding from a couple of glass cuts, but the seat belt had kept me from serious injury. I was vaguely concerned about the danger of fire, but the engine had died, and before long I heard the sound of sirens. I had just begun to wonder how much longer I'd be trapped inside when a couple of firemen helped me get out, and soon I was sitting on the curb, my aching head in my hands, my face and shirt dripping with blood.

That's when I got a good look at Dad's red pickup. It was scraped and dented and crushed, and I was surprised that I had walked away from it in one piece. And by then I was sort of wishing I hadn't, because it suddenly dawned on me that I would soon have to face Dad with some very bad news about one of his pride-and-joy cars.

We lived in a small town, and several people who saw the

accident knew me. Someone must have called Dad right away, because it wasn't long after I was rescued from the wreck that he came running up to me. I closed my eyes, not wanting to see his face.

"Dad, I'm so sorry—"

"Terry, are you all right?" Dad's voice didn't sound at all like I thought it would. When I looked up, he was on his knees next to me on the curb, his hands gently lifting my cut face and studying my wounds. "Are you in a lot of pain?"

"I'm okay. I'm really sorry about your truck."

"Forget the truck, Terry. The truck's a piece of machinery. I'm concerned about you, not the truck. Can you get up? Can you walk? I'll drive you to the hospital unless you think you need an ambulance."

I shook my head. "I don't need an ambulance. I'm fine."

Dad carefully put his hands under my arms and lifted me to my feet. I looked up at him uncertainly and was amazed to see that his face was a study in compassion and concern. "Can you make it?" he asked, and his voice sounded scared.

"I'm fine, Dad. Really. Why don't we just go home? I don't need to go to the hospital."

We compromised and went to the family doctor, who cleaned up my wounds, bandaged me, and sent me on my way. I don't recall when the truck got towed, what I did for the rest of that night, or how long I was laid up. All I know is that for the first time in my life, I understood that my father loved me. I hadn't realized it before, but Dad loved me more than his truck, more than any of his cars, more than I could have possibly imagined.

Since that day we've had our ups and downs, and I've disappointed him enough to make him mad, but one thing remains unchanging. Dad loved me then, he loves me now, and he'll love me for the rest of my life.

A wise woman once said to me:
"There are only two lasting bequests
we can hope to give our children.
One of these is roots; the other, wings."
— Hodding Carter

OF MORE VALUE

Jerry Jenkins

FROM *STILL THE ONE*

A friend, the father of two daughters, admits he doesn't mind putting a little fear into the boys. His daughters may be embarrassed when he asks for a few moments alone with their dates, and he might rather the young men think he's an okay guy than that he's a mean, protective father. But some things are worth a little awkwardness. Boys might think such dads are a little overprotective. To the fathers of daughters, however, there is no such thing as overprotective.

Another friend says he uses a sports car analogy to get his point across. He'll say to the boy, "If I owned the most expensive, exotic sports car on the road and I let you take it for a spin, you'd be careful with it, wouldn't you?"

"Oh, yes, sir, you bet."

"You'd treat it better than if it were your own, wouldn't you?"

"Yes, sir."

"I wouldn't want to think you were screeching the tires, would I?"

"No, sir."

"Well, let me tell you something, just so we're straight with each other, man to man. My daughter is of infinitely more value to me than any car could be. Do you get my drift? She's on loan from me to you for the next few hours, and I wouldn't want to discover that she was treated with any less care or respect than I would give her. I'm responsible for her. She's mine. I'm entrusting her to you. That trust brooks no second chances. Understand?"

By then, of course, the young man is wondering why he didn't ask someone else out. He's only nodding, unable to speak. Most often, he brings the girl home earlier than promised. The daughter might even complain about her father's approach, but deep down she feels loved and cherished, and you can be sure she'll marry a man who treats her that way.

My father never talked to me about how to treat people.
Every act of kindness I have ever shown another person
was because I was trying to imitate him.
—*Pamela McGrew*

JUST BEING THERE

I can remember times as my boys were growing up when one of them would be very troubled or worried or had endured a disappointment or hurt. Sometimes after he was in bed at night, I'd go and just lie down on the bed beside him. It's nice if you can think of wise, fatherly words in those moments, but the words aren't always there. It was enough just to lie beside my boy and be there with him.

Ron Mehl
FROM *THE CURE FOR A TROUBLED HEART*

LETTER TO A COACH
An Athlete's Dad

*D*ear Coach,

I just read your letter to my son and us (the parents) telling of your expectations for athletes under your tutelage. Johnny's mother and I couldn't agree more as we have long recognized the values deriving from high school athletics.

Judging from your record you must teach the game very well. That is important.

There is another phase of coaching, I believe, that is even more important. Permit me to explain what I mean.

Coach, John's mother and I are giving you our most prized possession to use for several weeks. During that time and throughout the next four years our son will make you one of our prime household conversations. He'll tell about how you could have made the Packers if only you hadn't hurt your knee back in '65. He'll tell us about your emotional halftime talk when you came from behind and beat Rivaltown. We'll hear about how you can still pass or kick the football. When we are hearing all this talk our son's eyes will shine. You see, Coach, he'll idolize you.

We don't have many heroes anymore. Many professionals would sell their souls for a buck it seems. Some college athletes made the news this year in a very negative manner. We know all college athletes don't shoplift, etc., but that is what we hear about.

You are our son's hero. We are relying on you. His muscles are nearly developed but his mind is still fragile and so impressionable. Your responsibilities are great. Impress him, Coach. Pour it on!

You don't raise heroes, you raise sons.
And if you treat them like sons, they'll turn out to be heroes,
even if it's just in your own eyes.
— *Walter Schirra*

ARE YOU WONDERING WHERE YOUR SON IS?

Tim Hansel

FROM *WHAT KIDS NEED MOST IN A DAD*

Throughout their lives my mother and dad quietly gave even when they didn't see the results. They both had to make numerous sacrifices as my brother and I were growing up. Mom and Dad both worked two jobs in order to help make ends meet.

My brother, Steve, was a fine student and president of his senior class. I tried to follow in his footsteps, although I had a wilder bent at times. I worked hard to be a good student and a good athlete. I even made student body president, which was partly due to some successes on the football field. In my senior year I was voted "All City" and "All State."

On the night of one of my greatest triumphs, however, I failed my father miserably, and it was then that he demonstrated his ability as a servant leader. We had just won our final football game, which meant that we would be going to the State Championship. Some of us had been informed that we would repeat as all league selections for a second year. We decided that all of this success was worth celebration. So many of us football players got together and truly celebrated—a bit too hard. Somewhere we had gotten some beer, and according to our high school logic, we thought that the more we drank the more we were celebrating. We drank too much.

A policeman happened to drive by and spot us in a parking lot behind some stores. Doing his job, he came over to investigate and discovered that more than a few of us were quite thoroughly inebriated.

The policeman put in a call for some help. Then, in my opinion, he started pushing around some of my friends. Because I was student body president, I felt it was my job to defend them and I ended up trying to wrestle with the cop. That was not a good idea.

The next thing the cop called for was a paddy wagon. Twenty minutes later we were all on our way to jail. That night was one of the longest I've ever spent. At about five the next morning—just about the time the newspaper was being delivered to our home with my picture in it for being an All City and All State athlete—my parents received a phone call from the chief of police.

"Mr. and Mrs. Hansel, are you wondering where your son is? I'm phoning from the city jail and I would like you to come down here and pick up your son."

I can imagine how long that drive downtown was for my folks. When they arrived, they saw a group of dejected young men. Other

parents also arrived and had to face the same kind of disappointment. Their sons, who just a few hours before had been a source of
such great pride, had all failed so miserably.

My mom and dad walked in and I'll never forget the moment
when their eyes met mine. They must have been wondering if all
their sacrifices had been worth it. But they never spoke a word.

We got in the car. The sun was coming up and tears were
rolling down my cheeks. Finally, I could take the silence no longer
and blurted, "Aren't you going to say something, Dad?"

After a pause that probably seemed longer than it really was,
my dad finally spoke. "Sure...let's go home and have some breakfast, son."

Those were the only words he uttered. At a time when I had
failed him most tragically, he reminded me that I was his son. At a
time when I felt the deepest remorse and a total failure, he said, in
effect, "Let's get on with it."

In the years that followed, he never once brought up that inci-
dent. He simply continued to love me for who I was and who I
could be.

A Super Dad? Not really. He had all kinds of rough edges and
some very real flaws.

A servant father? Indeed.

THE STORM
Tony Campolo

FROM *20 HOT POTATOES*

A friend of mine has an adorable four-year-old daughter. She is bright, and she is talkative. If tryouts were being held for a modern-day Shirley Temple, I think she would win, hands down.

One night there was a violent thunderstorm. The lightning flashed and the thunder rumbled—it was one of those terrifying storms that forces everyone to stop and tremble a bit. My friend ran upstairs to his daughter's bedroom to see if she were frightened and to assure her that everything would be all right. He got to her room and found her standing on the window sill, spread-eagled against the glass. When he shouted, "What are you doing?" she turned away from the flashing lightning and happily retorted, "I think God is trying to take my picture."

DRIVING LESSONS

Charles Swindoll

FROM *THE GRACE AWAKENING*

I remember when I first earned my license to drive. I was about sixteen, as I recall. I'd been driving off and on for three years (scary thought, isn't it?). My father had been with me most of the time during my learning experiences, calmly sitting alongside me in the front seat, giving me tips, helping me know what to do. My mother usually wasn't in on those excursions because she spent more of her time biting her nails (and screaming) than she did advising. My father was a little more easygoing. Loud noises and screeching brakes didn't bother him nearly as much. My grandfather was the best of all. When I would drive his car, I would hit things...*Boom!* He'd say stuff like, "Just keep on going, Bud. I can buy more fenders, but I can't buy more grandsons. You're learning." What a great old gentleman. After three years of all that nonsense I finally earned my license.

I'll never forget the day I came in, flashed my newly acquired permit, and said, "Dad, look!"

He exclaimed, "Whoa! Look at this. You got your license.

Good for you!" Holding the keys to his car, he tossed them in my direction and smiled, "Tell you what, son...you can have the car for two hours, all on your own." Only four words, but how wonderful: "All on your own."

I thanked him, danced out to the garage, opened the car door, and shoved the key into the ignition. My pulse rate must have shot up to 180 as I backed out of the driveway and roared off. While cruising along "all on my own," I began to think wild stuff—like, This car can probably do 100 miles an hour. I could go to Galveston and back twice in two hours if I averaged 100 miles an hour. I can fly down the Gulf freeway and even run a few lights. After all, nobody's here to say, "Don't!" We're talking dangerous, crazy thoughts! But you know what? I didn't do any of them. I don't believe I drove above the speed limit. In fact, I distinctly remember turning into the driveway early...didn't even stay away the full two hours. Amazing, huh? I had my dad's car all to myself with a full gas tank in a context of total privacy and freedom, but I didn't go crazy. Why? My relationship with my dad and my granddad was so strong that I couldn't, even though I had a license and nobody was in the car to restrain me. Over a period of time there had developed a sense of trust, a deep love relationship.

After tossing me the keys, my dad didn't rush out and tape a sign on the dashboard of the car, "Don't you dare drive beyond the speed limit" or "Cops are all around the city, and they'll catch you, boy, so don't even think about taking a risk." He simply smiled and said, "Here are the keys, son, enjoy it." What a demonstration of grace. And did I ever enjoy it!

The best way to keep kids at home is
to make the home a pleasant atmosphere...
and to let the air out of their tires.
—*Author unknown*

NINE WORDS

Never forget the nine most

important words of any family—

I love you.

You are beautiful.

Please forgive me.

H. Jackson Brown Jr.

FROM *LIFE'S LITTLE TREASURE BOOK ON*

MARRIAGE AND FAMILY

STANDING TALL

Steve Farrar

FROM *STANDING TALL*

When I was a sophomore in high school, we moved to a new town and a new high school. It was the typical scenario of being the new kid who didn't know anyone. One of the fastest ways to make friends in that situation is to go out for a sport. In about two days you know more guys from playing ball than you could meet in three months.

Normally, I would have gone out for basketball. But I had done something very foolish. I had brought home a "D" on my last report card. The only reason I had gotten a "D" was that I had horsed around in the class and basically exhibited some very irresponsible behavior in turning in papers. My dad had a rule for the three boys in our family, and the rule was this: if any of us got anything lower than a "C" in a class, we couldn't play ball. He didn't demand that we get straight "A's" or make the honor roll. My dad knew that the only reason any of us would get a "D" was that we were fooling around instead of acting in a responsible way.

As a result, I didn't go out for basketball. Now my dad was all for me playing ball. He had been all-state in both basketball and football in high school, went to college on a basketball scholarship, and after World War II, was offered a contract to play football for the Pittsburgh Steelers. He wanted me to play. But he was more interested in developing my character than he was in developing my jump shot. My dad had some long-term goals for me that were more important than basketball. He knew it would be very good for me to have to live with the consequence of sitting out a basketball season due to my lackadaisical behavior.

One day I was in my physical education class, and we were playing basketball. I didn't know it but the varsity coach was in the bleachers watching the pickup game. After we went into the locker room he came up to me and asked me who I was and why I wasn't out for varsity basketball. I told him that we had just recently moved into town and that I'd come out for basketball next year. He said that he wanted me to come out this year.

I told him that my dad had a rule about getting any grade lower than a "C."

The coach said, "But according to the school rules you're still eligible to play if you have just one 'D.'"

"Yes, sir, I realize that," I replied. "But you have to understand that my dad has his own eligibility rules."

"What's your phone number?" the coach asked. "I'm going to call your dad."

I responded, "I'll be happy to give you the phone number, but it will be a waste of your time."

This coach was a big, aggressive guy. He was about six feet two inches and 220 pounds which put him one inch shorter and twenty pounds lighter than my dad. Coach was used to getting his own way. But he hadn't met my dad. I knew before the coach ever called what my dad's answer would be.

Was my dad capable of change? Sure he was. Was he going to change because he got a call from the varsity coach? Of course not. A lot of dads would have been so flattered that they would have compromised on the consequences.

That night after dinner Dad told me the coach had called. He told me he had told the coach no. He then reminded me of the importance of being responsible in class and that he really wanted me to play basketball. But the ball was in my court (no pun intended). If I wanted to play ball it was up to me. At that point, I was very motivated to work hard in class so that I could play basketball the next season.

The next morning the coach came up to me in the locker room. "I talked to your dad yesterday afternoon and he wouldn't budge. I explained the school eligibility rules, but he wouldn't change his mind. I don't have very much respect for your father."

I couldn't believe my ears. This coach didn't respect my father. Even I had enough sense to know my dad was doing the right thing. Sure, I wanted to play ball but I knew my dad was a man of his word and he was right in not letting me play. I couldn't believe this coach would say such a thing.

"Coach," I said. "I can tell you that I highly respect my dad. And I also want you to know that I will never play basketball for you."

I never did. I got my grades up, but I never went out for varsity basketball. I refused to play for a man who didn't respect my dad for doing what was right. That was the end of my high school basketball career because the man coached basketball for my remaining years in high school.

Why wouldn't I play for him? Because he didn't respect my father. If he didn't have the sense to respect my dad then I sure as heck wasn't going to play for him. Come to think of it, the real reason I wouldn't join his team was that I didn't respect him. He was a compromiser and I suspected that he would do anything to win. My dad was a man of conviction and a man of character. And any coach who couldn't see that was not the kind of man I wanted to

associate with. My dad was strict and unwilling to change his conviction even though it hurt him for me not to play ball. My dad was
capable of change, but he was unwilling to change because he had a
long-term objective for my life that the coach didn't have.

The coach wanted to win games. My dad wanted to build
a son.

I have no greater joy than to hear
that my children walk in truth.
— 3 John 1 : 4

FINAL SEASON
Bob Welch

FROM *A FATHER FOR ALL SEASONS*

*T*he other night, after the parents had all come to pick up their sons and I was picking up catcher's equipment, bats and, of course, one forgotten mitt, it dawned on me that this was it: the last season I would coach one of my sons' baseball teams.

Two sons. Twelve seasons. Hundreds of games. Maybe three decent umps. And thousands of memories, hidden in my mind like all those foul balls lost in the creek behind the Ascot Park backstop.

Sitting in the rickety bleachers that spring evening—everyone had gone—I found myself lost in thought, mentally walking along the creek, finding those long-forgotten foul balls and listening to the stories they had to tell.

The time our left fielder got locked in a Dairy Queen bathroom during a postgame celebration. The time I handed a protective cup to our new catcher and he thought it was an oxygen mask. The time a T-baller cleanly fielded a grounder, picked it up and tossed it to his mom, who was sitting behind third base reading *Gone with the Wind*.

For something that became more than a decade-long family

affair, it had begun casually enough. While watching one of my five-year-old son's T-ball games in 1985, a manager asked if I would coach second base.

"Uh, second base?"

"Yeah. At this level you need coaches at second base or the kids will forget to take a left and wind up at Safeway."

So I coached second base. And before long, our family's summers revolved around a diamond: me coaching, my wife Sally keeping score, and the boys playing. Like the Israelites trudging out of Egypt, we hauled our equipment, lawn chairs, video cameras and sixty-four-ounce drinks from ballfield to ballfield, week after week, summer after summer.

The time our right fielder turned up missing during a championship game, only to be found at the snack bar eating licorice and flirting with girls. The time we showed up at an empty field, only to discover that I'd read the schedule wrong and our game was actually ten miles away.

The time I explained to my fifth-grade team that, because we'd given up eighty-nine runs in the last four games, we needed to set a defensive goal.

"It's a six-inning game," I explained. "Let's just try to hold them to twelve runs per game. Two per inning. Can you do that?"

Silence. Then my philosophical right fielder spoke up.

"Coach," he said, "do we have to give up the runs even like that, or could we like give up all twelve in the last inning?"

Our teams were more than a collection of kids. They were extended family, some of whom would end up sleeping overnight and going to church with us. And some of the boys desperately needed that. One year, of fifteen players, only five had a mother and father living together under the same roof. Once, a boy missed practice because his aunt had been murdered. And I can't count the number of times I took kids home because nobody came to pick them up.

But I've always remembered the advice I heard at a coaching clinic: "Who knows? The six hours a week you spend with a kid might be the only six hours that he actually feels loved."

The out-of-control coach who pushed me off the field. The kid who didn't get picked for my team firing a splat gun at our left fielder. The father who dropped off his son, Willie, and told him to get his own ride home; he and his girlfriend were going to a tavern to throw darts. We went into extra innings that afternoon, and the man's son played the game of his life, going all nine innings at catcher and making the game-winning hit.

We tried to make it more than just baseball. With help from our sons, we established a team newspaper. A few times I'd put candy in the sack at second base and let players dig in every time they threw out a runner. (Best defensive practice we ever had.)

Sally was our DH—designated healer—with her ever-present cooler of pop and packages of frozen corn for sprained ankles and bruised arms. Once, we had pizza delivered to the ballfield just after we'd lost to a team with one of those scream-and-yell coaches. I think we had more fun that night than the team that won.

The time we won with only eight players. The time Michael, a friend of my youngest son, spent the night at our house and played hours of backyard baseball, the rules stipulating that you must run the bases backward. The next morning, in a regulation game, Michael hit a hot grounder and promptly took off—for third base.

Over the years we won games, we lost games, and we lost baseballs—zillions of them. But for every ball we lost, we gained a memory. As a family, we laughed together, cried together, got dusty together—as if each of those hundreds of games was a microcosm of real life, which it was.

A weak-hitting kid named Cody stroking a three-run double and later telling his mom, "I'm trying to stop smiling, but I just can't."

My oldest son becoming my assistant coach and reaching a few kids in a way that I could not.

Kids I coached as third-graders now taller than I am.

And, of course, the night we were going to win the city championship. But for the first time in two months, it rained. Instead of playing on a field of dreams with perfectly straight white lines and a public address system, some official handed us a bunch of medals and called us cochamps.

Later that night, after the postseason pizza banquet, the restaurant manager approached me, broom in hand. "Excuse me, but are you the coach of the Washington Braves?"

"I sure am," I said, figuring he was going to pull me out of my doldrums by congratulating me on the cochampionship.

"Coach," he said, handing me the broom, "your team trashed the indoor play room. Wanna help sweep?"

Two sons. Twelve seasons. Hundreds of games. As a family, we had shared them all. But what, I wondered, had we missed in the process? What had we given up in order to pursue what some might see as trivia?

Nothing. Because whether your family is together at baseball games or camping trips or rodeos or dog shows or soccer tournaments or swim meets, the common denominator is this: families together—a rarity in our busy times—making memories. Learning lessons. Sowing seeds that can be nourished only by time.

Regrets? Only one. I wish Willie's father had considered his son more important than a game of darts. He missed seeing his teammates mob him after making the game-winning hit.

The time a tall third baseman was making fun of my 4-foot-9 son at the plate—until my son nearly took off his head with a line-drive double.

My oldest son proudly posing for pictures with his grandparents after the team won a city championship.

The time he played his final game and walking to the car afterward, it hit me like a line drive in the side of the head. This was it. I'd never coach him in baseball again.

Dusk was descending. It was time to head for home where my family—the boys were now seventeen and fifteen—would be. As I slung the equipment bag over my shoulder and walked down from the stands, I noticed a young father and his son playing catch between short and third.

I smiled slightly and headed for the car, leaving behind plenty of lost balls for others to find.

ENCOURAGEMENT

LOOK ALIKES
Linda Mango

REPRINTED WITH PERMISSION OF
THE READER'S DIGEST ASSOCIATION, INC.

*W*hile working at a medical center, I noticed a distinguished gentleman and his young son on their daily visits to the chemotherapy center. Impeccably tailored suit and a head of lush salt-and-pepper hair made the man stand out. As I admired him and his smiling five-year-old, I found it impossible to tell who was receiving treatment.

One day, as they walked past, my attention was drawn to the boy. The cap he usually wore was missing, and I could now see a shiny bald head. I turned toward the father. To my surprise, he was as bald as his son.

"Look at my dad!" the boy said cheerfully. "He shaved his head so we'd look the same. We're going to grow our hair back together!"

His father simply smiled, looking more distinguished than ever.

LOOK, DADDY, I CAN FLY!

Becky Freeman

FROM *STILL LICKIN' THE SPOON*

Although I love the slinky, silky gowns my husband gives me every holiday season, this year I asked if he might give me something a little less breezy. I was particularly interested in sleepwear that would wrap warm and snugly around my cold, cold feet.

Thinking it would be a cute joke, Scott gave me a pair of "woman size" pink and white feety pajamas—in a teddy bear print. Christmas evening, I stole away to the bedroom and tried them on just for fun. As I put one foot and then another into the pajama legs, I drifted back to the very first memory I have as a child. I could almost hear my daddy—as he sounded nearly thirty-five years ago—softly singing, "Put your little foot, put your little foot, put your little foot right here..." as I stood on my bed while he helped me into my feety pj's.

My father is one man who has managed, all his life, to keep his child-heart pumping strong.

One rainy spring afternoon, when I was about eleven, I went out to the garage to find my father ascending a ladder into the attic. Though Daddy was sentimental, he was not a handyman, so the sight of the ladder provoked my curiosity. Then he crooked his finger in a silent gesture that I knew meant, "Come along, but be quiet."

I followed him up into the attic and sat down beside him, curious as to the nature of our exploration. But all my dad said was, "Shhh...listen." Then I heard it. The rain, pattering overhead—amplified by our nearness to the rooftop.

"I come up here whenever it rains," Daddy said softly. It was cool and comforting, a tender moment caught—like a snapshot—in my mind.

To my pleasant surprise, my husband turned out to be a rain-on-the-roof kind of guy, too. He even built our bed so that the head of it fits snug against a large picture window. At night, if the full moon is shining or a soft rain is falling, Scott pulls up the blinds and raises the window and whispers, "Shhh...Becky. Listen." And this, I believe, is part of the reason why the two men I love most in the whole world are my daddy and my husband.

Another amazing thing about Daddy: In all my years, I cannot ever recall my father criticizing me. Not once. Always, he would praise and encourage my efforts—however crazy, however childish.

Not long ago I had a dream; it is a dream I've had for years. In it I can fly. I love these dreams, and while I'm in them, I cannot understand why other people don't just float themselves up to the sky and join me. It is so easy, nothing to it at all. Most of the time I just spread out my arms and take off, but in one of my dreams I piloted a Frisbee. Now that was fun!

But the last dream I had was especially realistic. Once again I was flying, and in my dream I thought to myself, This is ridiculous. Nobody else is flying except me. I need to find out if this is real or if this is just my imagination.

So I flew to my parents' home, knocked on the door, and floated up to the ceiling. Then I hovered over my father, who was looking up at me, not at all surprised to find me up there, and I said, "Daddy, listen. You've got to tell me the truth. I really think I'm flying. It feels so real. But I'm worried that this might just all be a dream."

My daddy's answer was swift and sure. "Honey," he said, "it's no dream. You're flying all right."

When I woke up I laughed, but then tears welled in my eyes. How marvelous, I thought, that even in my subconscious, in spite of all logic to the contrary, I have a father who believes I can fly.

For Father's Day last year, I could not find a card that seemed to fit how I felt about Daddy. However, I came across a scene in a children's book that turned out to be perfect. It was a scene with Piglet and Winnie-the-Pooh, walking side by side toward a setting sun. Their short conversation summed up exactly how I felt about my father through the years.

Piglet sidled up to Pooh from behind.

"Pooh!" he whispered.

"Yes, Piglet?"

"Nothing," said Piglet, taking Pooh's paw. "I just wanted to be sure of you."

My dad has been like Pooh to me, his Little Girl-Piglet. Oh, we don't chit-chat a whole lot, not like my mother and I anyway. But in every memory involving my father—from the time he sang, "Put your little foot" as he helped me into my feety pajamas, until this latest dream where he assured me that, yes, I could really fly—my father has been there in the shadows, cheering me on. He has given me the steadfast assurance that always, and forever, I can be sure of him.

SHADES OF LIGHT

*A*ffirming words from moms and dads are like light switches. Speak a word of affirmation at the right moment in a child's life and it's like lighting up a whole roomful of possibilities.

Gary Smalley and John Trent

DAD'S HELPER
Ron Mehl

FROM *THE CURE FOR A TROUBLED HEART*

A little boy was helping his father move some books out of an attic into more spacious quarters downstairs. It was important to this little boy that he was helping his dad, even though he was probably getting in the way and slowing things down more than he was actually assisting. But that boy had a wise and patient father who knew it was more important to work at a task with his young son than it was to move a pile of books efficiently.

Among this man's books, however, were some rather large study books, and it was a chore for the boy to get them down the stairs. As a matter of fact, on one particular load, the boy dropped his pile of books several times. Finally, he sat down on the stairs and wept in frustration. He wasn't doing any good at all. He wasn't strong enough to carry the big books down a narrow stairway. It hurt him to think he couldn't do this for his daddy.

Without a word, the father picked up the dropped load of

books, put them into the boy's arms, and scooped up both the boy and the books into his arms and carried them down the stairs. And so they continued for load after load, both enjoying each other's company very much. The boy carrying the books, the dad carrying the boy.

*The ultimate measure of a man
is not where he stands in moments
of comfort and convenience,
but where he stands at times of
challenge and controversy.*
— *Martin Luther King*

WORDS FOR YOUR FAMILY

Gary Smalley and John Trent

FROM *LEAVING THE LIGHT ON*

I'm proud of you.
Way to go!
Bingo—you did it.
Magnificent.
I knew you could do it.
What a good helper.
You're very special to me.
I trust you.
What a treasure.
Hurray for you!
Beautiful work.
You're a real trooper.
Well done.
That's so creative.
You make my day.

You're a joy.

Give me a big hug.

You're such a good listener.

You figured it out.

I love you.

You're so responsible.

You remembered.

You're the best.

You sure tried hard.

I've got to hand it to you.

I couldn't be prouder of you.

You light up my day.

My buttons are popping off.

I'm praying for you.

You're wonderful.

I'm behind you.

WHAT LITTLE GIRLS NEED

I knew I was special to him—that he was pulling for me and praying for me during each of the small crises that came my way. It's what every little girl needs from a father.

Danae Dobson
FROM *WHAT MY PARENTS DID RIGHT*

LESSONS IN BASEBALL

Chick Moorman

FROM *WHERE THE HEART IS*

As an eleven-year-old, I was addicted to baseball. I listened to baseball games on the radio. I watched them on TV. The books I read were about baseball. I took baseball cards to church in hopes of trading with other baseball card junkies. My fantasies? All about baseball.

I played baseball whenever and wherever I could. I played organized or sandlot. I played catch with my brother, with my father, with friends. If all else failed, I bounced a rubber ball off the porch stairs, imagining all kinds of wonderful things happening to me and my team.

It was with this attitude that I entered the 1956 Little League season. I was a shortstop. Not good, not bad. Just addicted.

Gordon was not addicted. Nor was he good. He moved into our neighborhood that year and signed up to play baseball. The kindest way of describing Gordon's baseball skills is to say that he didn't have any. He couldn't catch. He couldn't hit. He couldn't throw. He couldn't run.

87

In fact, Gordon was afraid of the ball.

I was relieved when the final selections were made and Gordon was assigned to another team. Everyone had to play at least half of each game, and I couldn't see Gordon improving my team's chances in any way. Too bad for the other team.

After two weeks of practice, Gordon dropped out. My friends on his team laughed when they told me how their coach directed two of the team's better players to walk Gordon into the woods and have a chat with him. "Get lost" was the message that was delivered, and "get lost" was the one that was heard.

Gordon got lost.

That scenario violated my eleven-year-old sense of justice, so I did what any indignant shortstop would do. I tattled. I told my coach the whole story. I shared the episode in full detail, figuring my coach would complain to the Little League office and have Gordon returned to his original team. Justice and my team's chances of winning would both be served.

I was wrong. My coach decided that Gordon needed to be on a team that wanted him—one that treated him with respect, one that gave everyone a fair chance to contribute according to their ability.

Gordon became my team member.

I wish I could say Gordon got the big hit in the big game with two outs in the final inning, but it didn't happen. I don't think Gordon even hit a foul ball the entire season. Baseballs hit in his direction (right field) went over him, by him, through him, or off him.

It wasn't that Gordon didn't get help. The coach gave him extra batting practice and worked with him on his fielding, all without much improvement.

I'm not sure if Gordon learned anything from my coach that year. I know I did. I learned to bunt without tipping off my intention. I learned to tag up on a fly if there were less than two outs. I learned to make a smoother pivot around second base on a double play.

I learned a lot from my coach that summer, but my most important lessons weren't about baseball. They were about character and integrity. I learned that everyone has worth, whether they can hit .300 or .030. I learned that we all have value, whether we can stop the ball or have to turn and chase it. I learned that doing what is right, fair and honorable is more important than winning or losing.

It felt good to be on that team that year. I'm grateful that man was my coach. I was proud to be his shortstop and his son.

TIME WITH DAD
Mary-Ellen Grisham

One day a girl of about five and her father came to the library before opening. I let them in early because the man explained he had an early doctor's appointment and would need to leave soon. He explained that the little girl just loved to come to the library and look at books and toys.

Even though I went about my usual work, I could hear the two of them moving about the library, looking and whispering. Finally I heard the little girl say, "I don't really like coming to the library as much as I like being with you." The man told the girl that she didn't need to make excuses; that she could come along with him whenever she liked.

I smiled as the two left the library, and thought to myself that the little girl's heart would most probably teach her as much as she would learn from books—or at least the most important truths anyway.

KINDNESS
Clark Cothern

FROM *AT THE HEART OF EVERY GREAT FATHER*

Ten-year-old Joseph Fisher learned a lesson on kindness when he almost ran over his dad with a tractor. Listen as Joe tells his story.

"I was breaking up some dirt one afternoon while my dad was working on a piece of equipment in the bar ditch on the north side of the field. The old Farmall tractor I was driving had to be turned by pulling a brake on one rear wheel or the other. If you applied the brake to the left wheel, the right wheel kept turning, so naturally, the tractor turned left. If you pulled the right brake, you turned right. It seems so obvious, but when you're ten...you sometimes forget these basic instructions.

"My dad was seated on the opposite side of the ditch, directly in front of where I was headed, and he was intent on his work, so he didn't see the big double wheels of the tractor until I pulled the wrong brake and started the tractor sliding in the wrong direction.

"I almost panicked, trying to stop the big old thing, but my dad jumped out of the way at the last minute, and the heavy front end of the tractor thumped to a stop right where Dad had been sitting.

"I expected him to come clean my plow (and not on the tractor), so I sat with my hands on the wheel, bracing myself for the explosion. Instead, he calmly walked up to me and asked, 'Are you okay?'

"I couldn't believe it. Here I was sitting on this huge tractor that I had almost steered right over my dad, and he asked if I was okay! When I told him I was fine, he simply said, 'Well, good. Do you know what you did wrong?' I told him, 'Yes, sir,' and he said, 'Great. There's a lesson you won't soon forget.' And he just smiled, patted my knee, and watched me drive the tractor back onto the field. Then he climbed back into the ditch and went back to work."

*The greatest thing in the world
is not so much where we stand as
in what direction we're moving.*
— Oliver Wendell Holmes

*There are many ways to measure success;
not the least of which is the way your child
describes you when talking to a friend.*

—*Author unknown*

INSPIRATION

A STREET VENDOR
NAMED CONTENTMENT

Max Lucado

FROM *NO WONDER THEY CALL HIM THE SAVIOR*

*A*hhh...an hour of contentment. A precious moment of peace. A few minutes of relaxation. Each of us has a setting in which contentment pays a visit.

Early in the morning while the coffee is hot and everyone else is asleep.

Late at night as you kiss your six-year-old's sleepy eyes.

In a boat on a lake when memories of a life well-lived are vivid.

In the companionship of a well-worn, dog-eared, even tearstained Bible.

In the arms of a spouse.

At Thanksgiving dinner or sitting near the Christmas tree.

An hour of contentment. An hour when deadlines are forgotten and strivings have ceased....

But unfortunately, in our squirrel cages of schedules, contests, and side-glancing, hours like these are about as common as one-legged monkeys. In our world, contentment is a strange street vendor, roaming, looking for a home, but seldom finding an open door.

This old salesman moves slowly from house to house, tapping on windows, knocking on doors, offering his wares: an hour of peace, a smile of acceptance, a sigh of relief. But his goods are seldom taken. We are too busy to be content....

"Not now, thank you. I've too much to do," we say. "Too many marks to be made, too many achievements to be achieved, too many dollars to be saved, too many promotions to be earned. And besides, if I'm content, someone might think I've lost my ambition."

So the street vendor named Contentment moves on.

My list of things was, for the most part, undone. My responsibilities were just as burdensome as ever. Calls to be made. Letters to be written. Checkbooks to be balanced.

But a funny thing happened on the way to the rat race that made me slip into neutral. Just as I got my sleeves rolled up, just as the old engine was starting to purr, just as I was getting up a good head of steam, my infant daughter, Jenna, needed to be held. She had a stomachache. Mom was in the bath so it fell to Daddy to pick her up.

She's three weeks old today. At first I started trying to do things with one hand and hold her with the other. You're smiling. You've tried that too? Just when I realized that it was impossible, I also realized that it was not at all what I was wanting to do.

I sat down and held her tight little tummy against my chest. She began to relax. A big sigh escaped her lungs. Her whimpers became gurgles. She slid down my chest until her little ear was right on top of my heart. That's when her arms went limp and she fell asleep.

And that's when the street vendor knocked at my door.

Good-bye, schedule. See you later, routine. Come back tomorrow, deadlines…hello, Contentment, come on in.

The Lord is near to all that call upon Him;
yea, He can feel breath when no voice can be heard for faintness.
— *John Trapp*

FAMILY PICTURE
Gary Rosberg

FROM *GUARD YOUR HEART*

was sitting in my favorite chair, studying for the final stages of my doctoral degree, when Sarah announced herself in my presence with a question: "Daddy, do you want to see my family picture?"

"Sarah, Daddy's busy. Come back in a little while, honey."

Good move, right? I was busy. A week's worth of work to squeeze into a weekend. You've been there.

Ten minutes later she swept back into the living room. "Daddy, let me show you my picture."

The heat went up around my collar. "Sarah, I said come back later. This is important."

Three minutes later she stormed into the living room, got three inches from my nose, and barked with all the power a five-year-old could muster: "Do you want to see it or don't you?" The assertive Christian woman in training.

"No," I told her, "I don't."

With that she zoomed out of the room and left me alone. And

somehow, being alone at that moment wasn't as satisfying as I thought it would be. I felt like a jerk. (Don't agree so loudly.) I went to the front door.

"Sarah," I called, "could you come back inside a minute, please? Daddy would like to see your picture."

She obliged with no recriminations and popped up on my lap.

It was a great picture. She'd even given it a title. Across the top, in her best printing, she had inscribed: "OUR FAMILY BEST."

"Tell me about it," I said.

"Here is Mommy [a stick figure with long yellow curly hair], here is me standing by Mommy [with a smiley face], here is our dog Katie, and here is Missy [her little sister was a stick figure lying in the street in front of the house, about three times bigger than anyone else]." It was a pretty good insight into how she saw our family.

"I love your picture, honey," I told her. "I'll hang it on the dining room wall, and each night when I come home from work and from class [which was usually around 10 P.M.], I'm going to look at it."

She took me at my word, beamed ear to ear, and went outside to play. I went back to my books. But for some reason I kept reading the same paragraph over and over.

Something was making me uneasy.

Something about Sarah's picture.

Something was missing.

I went to the front door. "Sarah," I called, "could you come back inside a minute, please? I want to look at your picture again, honey."

Sarah crawled back into my lap. I can close my eyes right now and see the way she looked. Cheeks rosy from playing outside. Pigtails. Strawberry Shortcake tennis shoes. A Cabbage Patch doll named Nellie tucked limply under her arm.

I asked my little girl a question, but I wasn't sure I wanted to hear the answer.

"Honey...there's Mommy, and Sarah, and Missy. Katie the dog is in the picture, and the sun, and the house, and squirrels, and birdies. But Sarah...where is your daddy?"

"You're at the library," she said.

With that simple statement my little princess stopped time for me. Lifting her gently off my lap, I sent her back to play in the spring sunshine. I slumped back in my chair with a swirling head and blood pumping furiously through my heart. Even as I type these words into the computer, I can feel those sensations all over again. It was a frightening moment. The fog lifted from my preoccupied brain for a moment—and suddenly I could see. But what I saw scared me to death. It was like being in a ship and coming out of the fog in time to see a huge, sharp rock knifing through the surf just off the port bow.

Sarah's simple pronouncement—"You're at the library"—got my attention big time.

God has any number of means at His disposal to slice through the haze and mist and get our attention. Are you letting Him get yours?

After He got mine—with my daughter's devastating family portrait—it took a couple of years before I finally celebrated "being home." It was a banner day for me as the three most important people in my life announced they had a gift for me. I smiled widely...until five-year-old Missy said it was a "drawing of our family." I know this sounds crazy, but my heart started thudding hard in my chest. There it was again, the wide-lined sheet of tablet paper festooned with colorful crayon figures, this time drawn by our youngest. My eyes scanned the family representation. There was Barbara with the yellow hair. There was Sarah. And Missy. And Katie the dog. And a big sun smiling down out of the sky.

And there was a tall guy with a mustache, standing smack in the middle of his family.

Daddy.

I was back in the picture. Back where I belonged. It was time to go out to 31 Flavors and celebrate with some big-time, double-dip cholesterol busters.

Missy's complete family picture still hangs over my desk in my counseling office. Each day as I work with hurting families needing hope, I keep that little portrait in the corner of my eye. It's a little reminder that I want to be in the picture from now on. But just like you, I have to renew that commitment every time the sun comes up on a new day. It never gets easy, but the payoff is bigger than I could have dreamed.

TESTAMENT

I have now disposed of all my property to my family. There is one thing more I wish I could give them, and that is the Christian religion. If they had that, and I had not given them one shilling, they would have been rich, and if they had not that, and I had given them all the world, they would be poor.

Patrick Henry

A   FATHER,   A   SON,
AND   AN   ANSWER
Bob Greene

*P*assing through the Atlanta airport one morning, I caught one of those trains that take travelers from the main terminal to their boarding gates. Free, sterile, and impersonal, the trains run back and forth all day long. Not many people consider them fun, but on this Saturday I heard laughter.

At the front of the first car—looking out the window at the track that lay ahead—were a man and his son. We had just stopped to let off passengers, and the doors were closing again. "Here we go! Hold on to me tight," the father said. The boy, about five years old, made sounds of sheer delight.

Most people on the train were dressed for business trips or vacations—and the father and son were dressed in clothes that were just about as inexpensive as you can buy.

"Look out there!" the father said to his son. "See that pilot? I bet he's walking to his plane." The son craned his neck to look.

As I got off, I remembered something I'd wanted to buy in the terminal. I was early for my flight, so I decided to go back. I did—and just as I was about to reboard the train for my gate, I saw that the man and his son had returned too. I realized then that they hadn't been heading for a flight, but had just been riding the shuttle.

"You want to go home now?" the father asked.

"I want to ride some more!"

"More?" the father said, mock-exasperated but clearly pleased. "You're not tired?"

"This is fun!" his son said.

"All right," the father replied, and when a door opened we all got on.

There are parents who can afford to send their children to Europe or Disneyland, and the children turn out rotten. There are parents who live in million-dollar houses and give their children cars and swimming pools, yet something goes wrong. Rich and poor, black and white, so much goes wrong so often.

"Where are all these people going, Daddy?" the son asked.

"All over the world," came the reply. The other people in the airport were leaving for distant destinations or arriving at the ends of their journeys. The father and son, though, were just riding this shuttle together, making it exciting, sharing each other's company.

So many troubles in this country—so many questions about what to do.

The answer is so simple: parents who care enough to spend time, and to pay attention, and try their best. It doesn't cost a cent, yet it is the most valuable thing in the world.

The train picked up speed, and the father pointed something out, and the boy laughed again, and the answer is so simple.

As for me and my household, we will serve the LORD.
—Joshua 24:15

YERR OUT!

Clark Cothern

FROM *AT THE HEART OF EVERY GREAT FATHER*

My father gave me a great example of self-control when I was a boy watching a church-league softball game.

Dad was forty-three at the time and very active. Though he wasn't known for hitting grand slams, he was good at placing the ball and beating the throw. Singles and doubles were his specialty, and he did the best he could with what he had.

This particular dusty, hot Phoenix evening, Dad poked a good one right over the second baseman's head, and the center fielder flubbed the snag and let the ball bloop between his legs.

My dad saw this as he rounded first base, so he poured on the steam. He was five feet ten inches, 160 pounds, and very fast. He figured that if he sprinted for third and slid, he could beat the throw.

Everyone was cheering as he sent two of his teammates over home plate. The center fielder finally got his feet under him and his fingers around the ball as Dad headed toward third. The throw came as hard and fast as the outfielder could fire it, and Dad started a long slide on that sunbaked infield. Dust flew everywhere.

The ball slammed into the third baseman's glove but on the other side of Dad—the outfield side—away from a clear view by the ump who was still at home plate. Our team's dugout was on the third base side of the diamond, and every one of the players had a clear view of the play.

Dad's foot slammed into third base a solid second before the ball arrived and before the third baseman tagged his leg. But much to the amazement—and then dismay—and then anger—of the team, the umpire, who hesitated slightly before making his call, yelled, "Yerr out!"

Instantly, every member of Dad's team poured onto the field and started shouting at once—Dad's teammates were intent on only one purpose: They wanted to win, and by golly they knew they were right!

The two runners who had crossed home plate before Dad was called out had brought the score to within one. If Dad was out— and we all knew he wasn't—his team was robbed of a single run.

With only one inning left, this one bad call could cost them the game.

But just as the fracas threatened to boil over into a mini-riot, Dad silenced the crowd. As the dust settled around him, he held up a hand. "Guys, stop!" he yelled. And then more gently, "There's more at stake here than being right. There's something more important here than winning a game. If the ump says I'm out, I'm out."

And with that, he dusted himself off, limped to the bench to get his glove (his leg was bruised from the slide), and walked back into left field all by himself, ready to begin the last inning. One by one, the guys on his team gave up the argument, picked up their own gloves, and walked out to their positions on the field.

I've got to tell you, I was both bewildered and proud that night. My dad's character was showing, and it sparkled. He may have been dusty, but I saw a diamond standing out there under the lights, a diamond more valuable than all the points his team might have scored.

For a few minutes that evening I was a rich kid, basking in my father's decision to be a man, to hold his tongue instead of wagging it, to settle the dust instead of settling a score. I knew his character at that selfless moment was worth more than all the gold-toned plastic trophies you could buy.

Dad held court that night and the verdict came down hard and he was convicted of being a man...and the evidence that proved it was his powerful use of that awe-inspiring weapon.

Self-control.

A SMALL BOY'S PRAYER
Rob Parsons
FROM SIXTY MINUTE FATHER

One night, when my son was small, I was saying prayers with him. The next day I was due to fly abroad to address an international law conference, and I was quite nervous. I've prayed many prayers for him, but this time asked him to pray for me. This is what he said: "Dear Lord, please help my Dad to be brave, and not to make too many mistakes." It's not a bad prayer for every father.

A FATHER'S PRAYER
OF ENLIGHTENMENT
John Ellis

ear heavenly Father, can you forgive me for hurting my children?

I came from a poor background so I thought that a big house would make my children feel important. I didn't realize that all it takes is my love.

I thought money would bring them happiness, but all it did was make them think that things were more important than people.

I thought spanking them would make them tough so that they could defend themselves. All it did was stop me from seeking wisdom so that I could discipline and teach them.

I thought that leaving them alone would make them independent. All it did was force my one son to be the father to my second son.

I thought that by smoothing over all of the family problems I was keeping peace. All I was teaching them was to run rather than lead.

I thought that by pretending to be the perfect family in public that I was bringing them respectability. All I was teaching them was to live a lie and keep the secret.

I thought that all I had to do to be a father was make money, stay at home, and supply all their material needs. All I taught them was that there is more to being a dad. The problem is they will have to guess what being a dad really is.

And dear God,

I hope you can read this prayer. My tears have smudged a lot of words.

O Lord...build me a son whose heart will be clear,
whose goal will be high; a son who will master himself
before he seeks to master other men;
one who will reach into the future, yet never forget the past.
— *General Douglas MacArthur*

FATHER'S DAY: A TRIBUTE

Max Lucado

FROM GOD CAME NEAR

oday is Father's Day. A day of cologne. A day of hugs, new neckties, long-distance phone calls, and Hallmark cards.

Today is my first Father's Day without a father. For thirty-one years I had one. I had one of the best. But now he's gone. He's buried under an oak tree in a west Texas cemetery. Even though he's gone, his presence is very near—especially today.

It seems strange that he isn't here. I guess that's because he was never gone. He was always close by. Always available. Always present. His words were nothing novel. His achievements, though admirable, were nothing extraordinary.

But his presence was.

Like a warm fireplace in a large house, he was a source of comfort. Like a sturdy porch swing or a big-branched elm in the backyard, he could always be found...and leaned upon.

During the turbulent years of my adolescence, Dad was one part of my life that was predictable. Girl friends came and girl friends went, but Dad was there. Football season turned into baseball season and turned into football season again and Dad was always there. Summer vacation, Homecoming dates, algebra, first car, driveway basketball—they all had one thing in common: his presence.

And because he was there life went smoothly. The car always ran, the bills got paid, and the lawn stayed mowed. Because he was there the laughter was fresh and the future was secure. Because he was there my growing up was what God intended growing up to be; a storybook scamper through the magic and mystery of the world.

Because he was there we kids never worried about things like income tax, savings accounts, monthly bills, or mortgages. Those were the things on Daddy's desk.

We have lots of family pictures without him. Not because he wasn't there, but because he was always behind the camera.

He made the decisions, broke up the fights, chuckled at Archie Bunker, read the paper every evening, and fixed breakfast on Sundays. He didn't do anything unusual. He only did what dads are supposed to do—be there.

He taught me how to shave and how to pray. He helped me memorize verses for Sunday school and taught me that wrong should be punished and that rightness has its own reward. He modeled the importance of getting up early and staying out of debt. His life expressed the elusive balance between ambition and self-acceptance.

He comes to mind often. When I smell Old Spice after-shave, I think of him. When I see a bass boat I see his face. And occasionally, not too often, but occasionally when I hear a good joke (the kind Red Skelton would tell), I hear him chuckle. He had a copyright chuckle that always came with a wide grin and arched eyebrows.

Daddy never said a word to me about sex or told me his life story. But I knew that if I ever wanted to know, he would tell me. All I had to do was ask. And I knew if I ever needed him, he'd be there.

Like a warm fireplace.

Maybe that's why this Father's Day is a bit chilly. The fire has gone out. The winds of age swallowed the late splendid flame, leaving only golden embers. But there is a strange thing about those embers, stir them a bit and a flame will dance. It will dance only briefly, but it will dance. And it will knock just enough chill out of the air to remind me that he is still…in a special way, very present.

If you take being a father seriously,
you'll know that you're not big enough for
the job, not by yourself. . . .
Being a father will put you on your
knees if nothing else ever did.

—ELISABETH ELLIOT
FROM *MARK OF A MAN*

ACKNOWLEDGMENTS

A diligent search has been made to trace original ownership, and when necessary, permission to reprint has been obtained. If I have overlooked giving proper credit to anyone, please accept my apologies. Should any attribution be found to be incorrect, the publisher welcomes written documentation supporting correction for subsequent printings. For material not in the public domain, grateful acknowledgment is given to the publishers and individuals who have granted permission for use of their material.

Acknowledgments are listed by story title in the order they appear in the book. For permission to reprint any of the stories please request permission from the original source listed below.

A TRIBUTE TO DAD

"What Kids Need" by Marty Wilkins, high school teacher, Milwaukie, OR. Used by permission. Marty is thankful for his wife, Becky, and his sons, Ryan, Taylor, and Caleb.

"The One the Father Loved Most" by Brennan Manning from *Lion and Lamb*, Chosen Books, a division of Baker Book House Company, © 1986. Used by permission.

"Dad Coming Home Was the Real Treat" by Howard Mann from the 16 June 1985 *Los Angeles Times*. Copyright 1985, Los Angeles Times. Reprinted by permission.

GROWING UP

"The Red Chevy" by T. J. Excerpted from *Sons: A Father's Love* by Bob Carlisle, © 1999, Word Publishing, Nashville, Tennessee. All rights reserved. Used by permission.

"Of More Value" by Jerry B. Jenkins from *Still the One*, published by Focus on the Family. Copyright © 1995 by Jerry B. Jenkins. All rights reserved. International copyright secured. Used by permission.

"Just Being There" by Ron Mehl from *The Cure for a Troubled Heart*, © 1996. Used by permission of Multnomah Publishers, Sisters, OR.

"Letter to a Coach" author and source unknown.

"Are You Wondering Where Your Son Is?" by Tim Hansel. Excerpt taken from *What Kids Need Most in a Dad* by Tim Hansel, Fleming H. Revell, a division of Baker Book House Company, © 1984. Used by permission.

ENCOURAGEMENT

"Shades of Light" by Gary Smalley and John Trent from *Leaving the Light On,* © 1994. Used by permission of Multnomah Publishers, Sisters, OR.

"Dad's Helper" by Ron Mehl from *The Cure for a Troubled Heart,* © 1996. Used by permission of Multnomah Publishers, Sisters, OR.

"Words for Your Family" by Gary Smalley and John Trent from *Leaving the Light On,* © 1994. Used by permission of Multnomah Publishers, Sisters, OR.

"What Little Girls Need" by Danae Dobson from *What My Parents Did Right,* published by Star Song Publishing Group © 1991. Used by permission of the author.

"Lessons in Baseball" by Chick Moorman from *Where the Heart Is: Stories of Home and Family* (Personal Power Press, Merrill, MI), © 1996. Used by permission of the author. For information on his newest book, *Parent Talk: Words that Empower, Words that Wound,* contact him at 1-800-797-4133.

"Time with Dad" (originally titled "A Way to Say I Love You") by Mary-Ellen Grisham "meg", © 1999. Used by permission.

"Kindness" by Clark Cothern from *At the Heart of Every Great Father,* © 1998. Used by permission of Multnomah Publishers, Sisters, OR.